BRUCE & STAN'S®
POCKET GUIDE TO

Knowing
Jesus

D1450287

BRUCE BICKEL and STAN JANTZ

HARVEST HOUSE PUBLISHERS
Eugene, Oregon 97402

Cover design by Left Coast Design, Portland, Oregon

Cover illustration by Krieg Barrie Illustrations, Hoquiam, Washington

Page 47—"One Solitary Life" as reproduced here was adapted from James A. Francis, *The Real Jesus and Other Sermons* (Philadelphia: The Judson Press, 1926), p. 123. Used by permission.

BRUCE & STAN'S® POCKET GUIDE TO KNOWING JESUS
Copyright © 2001 by Bruce Bickel and Stan Jantz
Published by Harvest House Publishers
Eugene, Oregon 97402

Library of Congress Cataloging-in-Publication Data

Bickel, Bruce, 1952–
   Bruce & Stan's pocket guide to knowing Jesus / Bruce Bickel and Stan Jantz.
     p. cm.
   Includes bibliographical references.
   ISBN 0-7369-0758-0
   1. Jesus Christ—Person and offices. 2. Theology, Doctrinal—Popular works.
I. Title: Bruce & Stan's pocket guide to knowing Jesus. II. Title: Pocket guide to knowing Jesus. III. Jantz, Stan, 1952- IV. Title.

BT203 .B53 2001
232—dc21   2001024259

Printed in the United States of America.

01 02 03 04 05 06 07 08 09 / BP-MS / 10 9 8 7 6 5 4 3 2 1

Contents

A Note from the Authors

Our culture is fascinated by famous people. That explains the popularity of celebrity interview shows like Leno's *Tonight Show* or Letterman's *Late Show*, or the *Live with Regis and Whoever* show. And don't forget about the plethora of cable shows devoted to nothing but biographies, such as, well, *Biography*, or the profile shows on E!, A&E, and the History Channel. And we've got magazines that focus on nothing else but people—like, well, *People*. Whether these folks are famous, or infamous, or just have an interesting story, we want to get "up close and personal" and find out their "behind-the-scenes" lives.

In our humble but correct opinion, there is no more fascinating person than Jesus Christ. Think about the promotional "teasers" that could be used to advertise a program about His life:

✓ He never went to college, yet some say He was the wisest man who ever lived. Who was this Jesus Christ: a country bumpkin or a cosmic brainiac?

✓ He was a loner with only a few friends, yet millions now claim to love Him. What made Him more attractive after His death than before?

✓ With absolutely no medical training, He gave sight to the blind, healed the lame, and brought the dead back to life. Was He a miracle man or just a charlatan in shepherd's clothing?

✓ He criticized the religious leaders of His day, yet He is the central focus of many worldwide religions. Hero or hypocrite?

✓ Just the son of a poor carpenter, He claimed to be the descendant of royalty. What is He: pauper or prince?

And these are just a few of the grabbers that could be used by legitimate biography shows. Imagine how the headlines of the supermarket tabloids would lead into a story about Jesus: "CHRIST CLAIMS TO BE LOVE CHILD OF VIRGIN AND OUTER SPACE ALIEN!" (On second thought, try *not* to imagine the tabloid headlines.)

You get our point. The evidence seems to present Jesus as an enormous enigma. As scholar C.S. Lewis has indicated about Jesus, either He was a liar, a lunatic, or the Lord.

This Book Is for You If...

Have you ever wondered about who Jesus really was (or is)? Do you want to get past the religious and ceremonial hype and get to know the real man (or God, or whatever He was)? If so, then you are our kind of people. In fact, we wrote this book especially for you if . . .

- ✓ You've got some legitimate questions about Jesus, but you can't ask any of your "religious" friends because you want some honest answers and not just more of the company line.

- ✓ There are things about Jesus that don't make sense to you. You don't raise your objections at church for fear of being laughed at or labeled a heretic.

- ✓ You've got no problem with Jesus. You think He was an okay guy. But you sure can't figure out why everyone has been making such a fuss about

Him for the last 2000 years. Hey, even Elvis has left the building, so you're wondering why people won't let Jesus do the same thing.

✓ You *do* have a problem with Jesus. Where does He get off claiming to be the only way to God? Who died and made Him God? Why should He have exclusive franchise rights to heaven?

Here's How We Can Help

So you want to know more about Jesus. Great, we are here to help. But our task is a little bit more difficult than making the usual introductions:

Bruce & Stan say: Hey, Jesus—You got a minute? We'd like to introduce You to one of our good friends, [insert your name here]. We think the two of you are really gonna hit it off.

You say: Jesus, sir! It is such an honor to meet You. You are so much bigger than I imagined.

Jesus says: I'm bigger than I imagined too. But there's an interesting story behind all of that. Let me tell you about it over a Starbuck's latte. But you'll have to treat. I don't carry a wallet. These robes never have a pocket.

No, it won't go anything like that. But we like to keep things on that level of informality at least. So, from time to time, we'll put an icon in the margin as a helpful hint to what we're talking about. Here's what they mean.

Big Idea—Pretty much everything about Jesus is important. But we know you can get distracted or lose your concentration as you are reading. So when you see this icon, pay close attention and doze off elsewhere.

Key Verse—Most of our information about Jesus comes straight from the Bible. Why? Because the Bible contains the statements that Jesus made about Himself and the stories that were written by people who lived with Him. All of the Bible verses are important, but this icon identifies the more famous ones.

It's a Mystery—There are some aspects of Jesus that are easy to understand. There are other things about Him that are incomprehensible. We don't have all the answers. (We know that comes as no great shock to those of you who have read our other books.) But neither does anyone else when it comes to knowing Jesus. Some things about Him remain a mystery, and we use this icon to admit it.

Glad You Asked—If you have some lingering questions about Jesus, we think we know what some of them are (because we had them too). We use this icon when we try to anticipate your questions.

Learn the Lingo—There is no life that has been studied more than Jesus. With all that brainpower devoted to analyzing Him, a lot of theological terminology has developed. We try to steer clear of words we can't pronounce or spell, so we won't try to impress you with the lingo. But every once in a while, we'll use this icon to identify a term that has particular relevance.

Dig Deeper—At the end of every chapter, we will refer you to a few other books that can give you even more information.

A Final Thought

There might be a lot of famous people that you are anxious to know. Most of them probably aren't interested in knowing you. But Jesus is the only One who died so that the two of you could know each other.

CHAPTER 1

THE PERSON OF JESUS: WHY IS HE SO SPECIAL?

If Jesus Christ were to come today, people would not even crucify him. They would ask him to dinner, and hear what he had to say, and make fun of it.

—Thomas Carlyle

BRUCE & STAN SAY

In many biographies, the most interesting part is *what* the person did. With Jesus, there is a lot of *what* to investigate. Some historians credit Him with starting a revolution that led to the downfall of the Roman Empire. Other people discount the conspiracy theories but recognize Jesus as a great philosopher and moral teacher. And don't forget about those reports that He performed supernatural feats, like walking on water and bringing dead people back to life (the kind of stunts that even David Blaine and David Copperfield won't attempt).

Before we look at *what* he did (we'll get to that in Chapter 2), we're going to look at *who* He was. With Jesus, that's the more intriguing question. If He was just a regular guy, then you've got to wonder how He pulled off all of that miracle stuff and why so many people claim allegiance to Him after all of these years. If He was God or something close to it, then why would He bother taking on a Clark Kent disguise as a mild-mannered human? See what we mean?

Don't think that you can skip this chapter. The answer may not be as simple as you expect.

Bruce & Stan

Chapter 1

The Person of Jesus:
Why Is He So Special?

*O*f all of the people who have ever lived, only a few have achieved permanent, worldwide notoriety. Most folks are known only to their friends, family, neighbors, and creditors. Some reach celebrity status, but that fame fades quickly (just ask Jaleel White, the guy who played Urkel on the now defunct *Family Matters* television show). Even those who attain the rank of hero are known only in a particular region. (George Washington means something to you but not to the residents of Tibet.)

Before you read any further, make a list of all of the people you can name who are known around the world and will be remembered throughout history.

Now take your list and eliminate the ones whose renown stems from their heinous deeds, such as Attila the Hun and Hitler the Nazi. (We know you didn't really make a list, but we'll pretend that you did.) We suspect that there aren't many names on your list, but Jesus probably made the cut.

What is it about Jesus that made Him such a prominent historical figure?

- ✓ It has nothing to do with money or fame, because as an adult He was basically homeless and lived in relative obscurity.

- ✓ It is something more than philosophy, because most philosophers are remarkably unknown.

✓ It isn't that He died as a martyr,
   because the graveyards are full of
   people who died for the sake of a
   cause.

✓ And it goes beyond religion, because
   other religious leaders haven't
   attained His prominence.

Something about Jesus has captured the
allegiance of people in every generation
since His death 2000 years ago. There was
something about Him that made Him
unique.

Jesus Claimed a Divine Distinction

Most of the identifiable aspects of Jesus
haven't made Him unique in history:

✓ He wore long hair and sandals, but so
   did the rest of the population of the
   Middle East in the first century (not to
   mention college students in the early
   1970s).

✓ He attracted large crowds wherever
   He went, but so did the Beatles and
   the Oscar Meyer wiener wagon.

✓ He did things that seemed to defy the laws of nature, but so did Michael Jordan on the basketball court.

✓ He has loyal followers who are ridiculed for their "misguided" allegiance, but the same can be said of anyone who uses an Apple computer.

But there is one thing that separates Jesus from the rest of us:

He claimed to be God!

He didn't say He was *like* a god. He said that He *was* God. When referring to God the Father, Jesus said it bluntly:

The Father and I are one (John 10:30).

It is doubtful that Jesus made this bold statement in jest or in a desperate attempt to grab a few headlines in the *Galilee Gazette*. The Jewish religious leaders considered such a claim as heresy, and they plotted His death because of it:

So the Jewish leaders tried all the more to kill him. In addition to disobeying the Sabbath rules, he had spoken of God as his

Father, thereby making himself equal with God (John 5:18).

Jesus wasn't the only one who believed that He was God with the power to forgive sin. So did John the Baptist:

The next day John saw Jesus coming toward him and said, "Look! There is the Lamb of God who takes away the sin of the world!" (John 1:29).

The belief that Jesus was God is a major theme of the New Testament. The apostle Paul, who wrote about half the books of the New Testament, summed it up like this:

For in Christ the fullness of God lives in a human body (Colossians 2:9).

This single distinction—the claim of Jesus to be God—has made Christ one of the central figures in all history. This "Jesus is God" premise is the foundation of Christianity. Any investigation of Jesus must begin with this question: Was He God or man?

WHAT A THING TO SAY!

Don't you find it interesting that there is no such inquiry about the other founders of major world religions? No one asks the "God or man?" question about Buddha, Confucius, or Mohammed. These men are known primarily for what they taught, and no one doubts that they were mere humans. (Their decaying corpses are proof of that.) But while Jesus is famous for His teaching, He is even more famous for His claims to be God. In fact, that claim is the central belief of Christianity. If His bones could be found in some grave, then the debate could be easily ended. But the grave was found empty. So we will have to look to other evidence.

Jesus Had the Proof to Back Up His Claim

Not only did Jesus claim to be God, He also played the part. He assumed the role that only God could perform when He pronounced that He was forgiving the sins of the people. One day He was preaching to a standing-room-only crowd when several men lowered their paralyzed friend down through the roof to be healed by Jesus. Here is how the episode is reported in the Gospel of Mark:

*Seeing their faith, Jesus said to the para-
lyzed man, "My son, your sins are
forgiven." But some of the teachers of religious law who were sitting there said to
themselves, "What? This is blasphemy!
Who but God can forgive sins!" Jesus
knew what they were discussing among
themselves, so he said to them, "Why do
you think this is blasphemy? Is it easier to
say to the paralyzed man, 'Your sins are
forgiven' or 'Get up, pick up your mat,
and walk'? I will prove that I, the Son of
Man, have the authority on earth to
forgive sins." Then Jesus turned to the
paralyzed man and said, "Stand up, take
your mat, and go on home, because you are
healed!" The man jumped up, took the
mat, and pushed his way through the
stunned onlookers* (Mark 2:5-12).

We know what you might be thinking:
"Claiming to possess the power to forgive
sins doesn't prove that Jesus was God.
Anyone can say that he is forgiving sins.
That's easy because there is no way to
ascertain whether or not it happened." We
agree. That's a good objection (and that's
apparently why Jesus healed the paralyzed
man—to show that He had supernatural
powers that only God possesses).

The healing of the paralyzed man wasn't a fluke. Jesus consistently exhibited powers and qualities that only belong to God:

- ✓ He gave sight to the blind (Mark 8:22-26).

- ✓ He cured the lame (John 5:1-9).

- ✓ He healed the sick (Luke 7:1-10).

- ✓ He raised the dead to life (Matthew 9:18-26).

- ✓ He fed thousands with only a boy's lunch (Matthew 14:14-21).

- ✓ He calmed a raging storm with one command (Matthew 8:23-27).

Throughout the New Testament, Jesus is described as having qualities only God can possess. In various passages, Jesus is described as being:

- ✓ Eternal (John 17:5)

- ✓ All-knowing (John 16:30)

- ✓ All-powerful (John 5:19)

- ✓ Unchangeable (Hebrews 13:8)

✓ The Creator of the Universe (Colossians 1:16)

Anyone can make an empty claim to be God. Jesus is the only one who has ever claimed to be God and who could deliver the power as proof to back it up.

He Had the Endorsement of God the Father

We each have a son in college (Matt is Bruce's son, and Scott is Stan's son). We are proud of our progeny, and we hope that the converse is true (although we may be operating under the self-serving misconception that we are cool dads). What would be the best substantiation for a claim by Matt and Scott that they are our sons (if they were ever inclined to admit it)? Wouldn't the best proof be our admission that we are their fathers? That same logic applies to Jesus who God acknowledged was His Son.

THE MYSTERY OF THE THREE-IN-ONE

Please excuse us if our discussion of Jesus being God and the Son of God seems a little confusing. It isn't our fault. Any discussion on this topic involves the mysterious concept of the Trinity—the three-in-one nature of God.

The word *trinity* doesn't even appear in the Bible, but it is an important aspect about God. The Trinity refers to the three distinct Persons which make up God:

- God the Father,

- Jesus Christ the Son, and

- the Holy Spirit.

Trinity does not mean that there are three gods who exist together to make up one God. There is only one God, but within that unity are three eternal and coequal Persons—all sharing the same essence and substance, but each having a distinct existence.

God the Father announced that Jesus was His Son in a booming voice from heaven when Jesus was baptized by John ("the Baptist").

After his baptism, as Jesus came up out of the water, the heavens were opened and he saw the Spirit of God descending like a dove and settling on him. And a voice from heaven said, "This is my beloved Son, and I am fully pleased with him" (Matthew 3:16,17).

This scene is incredible for two reasons:

✓ First, it reveals the three Persons of the Trinity present in one place at one time, distinct yet united: God the Father's voice is heard, Jesus Christ the Son is being baptized, and the Holy Spirit appears in the form of a dove.

✓ Secondly, and most pertinent to our discussion, God the Father is identifying Jesus as being His Son.

You can't get a better endorsement than from God Himself.

Jesus: The Messiah That No One Was Expecting

All throughout the Old Testament, God promised the Jews that He would send a king who would establish God's kingdom on earth. The "deliverer" was referred to as the Messiah. He would be God coming down to earth.

Whenever the Jews were in trouble, they were anxious for God to send relief:

- ✓ When the Jews were enslaved in Egypt, they cried out to God to rescue them. (Read Exodus 2:23.)

- ✓ When the nation of Israel was captured and its citizens exiled to Assyria or Babylonia, they were pleading with God to send the Messiah to rescue them. (Read Isaiah and the other prophets.)

- ✓ And when Israel was under the rule of the Roman government, the persecuted Jews were eagerly awaiting the Messiah to free them from their political bondage. As the Bible reads in Luke 3:15:

  Everyone was expecting the Messiah to come soon.

There was a big mystery surrounding the Messiah. Although they knew He was coming (because God had promised), the

Jews weren't sure how they would know who He was, and they didn't know when exactly He would arrive. But through the predictions in the Old Testament (called "prophecies" because the "prophets" were the ones that announced them), the Jews had some fairly specific clues about this Messiah guy. Here is a portion of the checklist that they were working from:

- ✓ *City of birth:* He was going to be born in the little town of Bethlehem (Micah 5:2). Apparently no one thought of checking the Bethlehem maternity ward on a daily basis to screen the babies for their Messiah-ship potential.

- ✓ *Parentage:* He would be a direct descendant of the famous King David (Isaiah 11:1).

- ✓ *Distinguishing characteristics:* As strange as it seems, the Messiah would be born to a virgin (Isaiah 7:14). How inconceivable!

- ✓ *Childhood:* Although born in Bethlehem, He would spend His childhood in Egypt (Hosea 11:1).

✓ *Notoriety:* He would have a ceremonial entrance into Jerusalem on a donkey (Zechariah 9:9). A rather humble and inauspicious ceremony for a Messiah, don't you think?

✓ *Death:* He would die by crucifixion, the method of death reserved for the most heinous criminals (Psalm 34:20).

✓ *Famous last words:* Even the Messiah's last, dying words were predicted (Psalm 22:1).

✓ *Resurrection from the dead:* As if the immaculate conception thing wasn't enough, the Messiah was predicted to come back to life after His death (Psalm 16:9,10).

Over the centuries, as the list of prophecies about the Messiah became longer, the pool of potential candidates got smaller. That doesn't mean that the Jews didn't have their share of Messiah impostors. Similar to Elvis impersonators, the counterfeits were easy to spot. Oh, maybe they could fake a few of the criteria (forging a birth certificate to show Bethlehem, riding a donkey into Jerusalem, etc.) but the impostors weren't willing to be crucified, and none of them could pull off the "come back to life after death" prediction.

What Are the Odds?

Bible scholars have identified more than 40 prophecies in the Bible concerning the Messiah that were made over a time span of several hundred years. The odds of any one person fulfilling all of those prophecies are astronomical. A statistician has calculated the odds and illustrated them with an analogy of finding one particular silver dollar out of 7.5 trillion cubic feet of silver dollars (about the same number of coins that it would take to cover the entire state of Texas three feet deep in silver dollars).

But along came Jesus Christ. He claimed to be the long-awaited Messiah. And He had the résumé to back it up:

✓ Born in Bethlehem—Luke 2:4,6,7

✓ A descendant of King David—Luke 1:31-33

✓ Born of a virgin (which was very hard to fake)—Matthew 1:18,22,23

✓ Raised in Egypt—Matthew 2:13-21

✓ Rode into Jerusalem on a donkey (the Palm Sunday parade)—Matthew 21:2, 4,5

✓ Famous last words—Mark 15:34

✓ Died on a cross—Matthew 27:32-35

✓ Came back to life (perhaps the hardest to fake)—John 20–21

No person before or after Christ has been able to pass the Messiahship test—only Christ.

Seven weeks after Jesus' resurrection, the religious leaders and the Roman authorities were still trying to quash the reports of Jesus' resurrection. People were beginning to realize that Jesus was the Messiah. If the Jewish and Roman authorities could have shown that Jesus failed to satisfy even one of the prophecies about the Messiah, they would have been glad to do so. But they couldn't. That is why no one challenged the disciple Peter when he stood in front of a crowd and preached a sermon that concluded with this statement:

> *So let it be clearly known by everyone in Israel that God has made this Jesus whom*

you crucified to be both Lord and Messiah!
(Acts 2:36).

Why Did Everyone Miss the Clues?

It seems so obvious that Jesus was the
Messiah (especially since He capped it off
by fulfilling the prophecies about the
details of the death and resurrection of the
Messiah). So why did almost everybody
miss it? How could they be so blind?

Most of the Jews expected the Messiah to
be a political, economic, and military king
who would lead them out of the oppression of the Roman authorities. When Jesus
came on the scene, stating that He was the
Messiah, the people were disappointed
because He preached about a spiritual
kingdom. He said that a change in the attitude of the heart was more important than
a change of the government.

The Jewish religious leaders might have
suspected that Jesus was the real Messiah,
but they didn't want to admit it. They
opposed Jesus because He had pointed out
their hypocritical religiosity. He said that a
relationship with God was dependent upon
the attitude of the heart, not on performing

religious ceremonies. Those religious leaders were big on ceremony, but they were weak on the loving God part. They didn't want to have anything to do with a Messiah like Jesus.

Jesus Was Just Like Us... Only Different

Have you ever wondered what God would look like? Is it difficult for you to get a mental picture of Him? God knew that we mere mortals would have a difficult time conceptualizing anything of a metaphysical nature, so He sent Christ to be a tangible presence of God on earth. That's the explanation that the apostle Paul used when he described Jesus Christ:

> *Christ is the visible image of the invisible God* (Colossians 1:15).

Jesus was God in a bod. It doesn't sound very glamorous or esoteric when we say it that way, but it is what the Bible says. Jesus was God.

WHAT DO YOU THINK?

This is a pop quiz, but it consists of only one multiple-choice question.

Jesus Christ was...

A) All-God (stuffed into human skin like some kind of holy sausage)

B) All-man (with periodic superhuman powers, like when a mother can lift up a car that has rolled onto her child)

C) Half-God and Half-man (and He could switch back and forth, sort of like Dr. Jekyll and Mr. Hyde)

D) None of the above

Based on what you've read so far in this chapter, you might think that "A" is the obvious answer to our little pop quiz. Well, don't be so sure of yourself. In fact, as you read the next few pages, you might be tempted to change your answer (but there would be no point to that because we aren't going to grade the quiz).

Jesus Was All-Human, Just Like Us

Even though Jesus declared Himself to be God, the Bible describes Jesus Christ being all-man. In fact, Jesus referred to Himself as "the Son of Man" (Luke 19:10). He frequently used this phrase in reference to Himself because He saw Himself as the representative for the human race. He identified Himself as being human.

Jesus also identified His ancestry as human. He referred to Himself as the son of David because He was born into the bloodline of Israel's famous king.

But the greatest evidence of His humanity is not what He said about Himself. His humanity is revealed in His life. Jesus Christ had traits that proved His humanity. Most significant of all, He had a body. This is obvious because so many people saw Him and touched Him. They couldn't nail a spirit to the cross. And His body had all of the traits that come with a human body (and which don't belong to a spirit):

✓ Jesus got hungry (Matthew 4:2).

✓ Jesus got thirsty (John 19:28).

✓ Jesus grew weary (John 4:6).

✓ Jesus experienced human love and compassion (Matthew 9:36).

✓ Jesus cried (John 11:35).

✓ Jesus was tempted (Hebrews 4:15).

These are the characteristics of a human. If Jesus was all-God just stuffed into human skin, then He could have existed on earth as a type of cyborg in human form without human feelings. But that isn't how it was. He had all of the human emotions and was just like we are...except for one major difference.

Everything About Him Was Human... Except for the Sin Part

Yes, Jesus was all-human, with one major—very major—distinction from the rest of us. He was sinless. That means that He never did anything that displeased God or violated the Mosaic Law. At every stage of His life (infancy, boyhood, adolescence, and manhood), He was holy and without sin.

Jesus must have considered Himself to be sinless. He was a Jew, and it was customary for all Jews to offer sacrifices for their sins. But there is no record of Jesus ever offering a single sacrifice, even though He was frequently in the temple. He didn't need to. He was without sin.

Perhaps the best proof of His sinlessness was demonstrated at the trials preceding His crucifixion. The religious authorities would have loved to present evidence that He had broken a law—religious or civil— but He hadn't. He was declared innocent 11 times:

- ✓ Six times by Pilate (Matthew 27:24; Luke 23:14,22; John 18:38; 19:4,6)

- ✓ Once by Herod (Luke 23:15)

- ✓ Once by Pilate's wife (Matthew 27:19)

- ✓ Once by the repentant thief (Luke 23:41)

- ✓ Once by a Roman centurion (Matthew 27:54)

- ✓ Once by Judas (Matthew 27:4)

There is further reliable proof that Jesus was without sin. As we will explain in Chapter 3, Jesus died for our sins. He could only be an acceptable sacrifice if He was sinless. All of Christianity is premised on that fact. The disciples—who knew Christ better than anyone—would not have been willing to be persecuted for their faith if they knew Christ was guilty of sin and if Christianity was based on a faulty premise. But these disciples declared Christ's holiness. Peter said it plainly:

He [Jesus] never sinned (1 Peter 2:22).

The disciple John echoed the same truth:

And you know that Jesus came to take away our sins, for there is no sin in him (1 John 3:5).

And the apostle Paul summed it up this way:

For God made Christ, who never sinned, to be the offering for our sin, so that we could be made right with God through Christ (2 Corinthians 5:21).

Why We Need Jesus to Be a Real Human

Are you a bit disappointed that Jesus was all-human? Well, don't be. Take comfort in the fact that Jesus knows from personal experience all about the struggles and hurts and stress of being a human. Because He was all-human, He can relate to us because He knows what we are going through.

> *This High Priest of ours [Jesus] under-*
> *stands our weaknesses, for he faced all of*
> *the same temptations we do, yet he did not*
> *sin. So let us come boldly to the throne of*
> *our gracious God. There we will receive his*
> *mercy, and we will find grace to help us*
> *when we need it* (Hebrews 4:15,16).

So, What Is He? God or Man?

Let's go back to the pop quiz from page 33. Has your answer to that question changed? Was Jesus: A) all-God, B) all-man, C) half and half, or D) none of the above?

Let's analyze the possibilities:

A) This can't be the right answer because we know that Jesus was all-human (except for the sin part).

B) This can't be the correct answer
   because we know that Jesus was all-
   God.

C) He wasn't a half-and-half. He had all
   the traits of humanity, and He had all
   the traits of God. He didn't have 50
   percent of each.

D) This is it! Jesus was none of the above,
   because He was A) and B) combined.

How is it possible that Jesus could be all-
God and all-man at the same time? No one
knows (although theologians give it the
fancy name of "hypostatic union"). But
that's exactly how the Bible describes
Jesus—as all-God and all-man at the same
time. It was an interesting balance:

✓ *His deity wasn't limited by His humanity.*
   He was always God, as evidenced by
   His sinlessness and supernatural
   powers.

✓ *His humanity wasn't overshadowed by
   His deity.* He didn't use His God
   powers to make His life easier. He
   experienced all the emotions that we
   have. He even endured the pain and
   suffering of the cross.

Jesus didn't give up His godly attributes. He simply took on human attributes as well.

Though he was God, he did not demand and cling to his rights as God. He made himself nothing; he took the humble position of a slave and appeared in human form (Philippians 2:6,7).

In His earthly body, He voluntarily chose not to use all His godly powers. When He was hungry, He didn't turn the stones into bread. But He could have. When He was being nailed to the cross, He didn't call down angels to rescue Him. But He could have. Choosing not to use an ability is different from not having it. And He had it all: all-man and all-God.

What's That Again?

1. Jesus was all-God. He made that claim about Himself, and He did the things that only God can do. Even God the Father declared that Jesus was His Son.

2. Jesus was the Messiah. He is the only person who has fulfilled every one of the prophecies about the Messiah.

3. Jesus was all-man. He knows everything that we are experiencing because He was a human just as we are (except He never sinned).

4. Jesus was all-God and all-man at the same time. He didn't lose any part of His God nature by becoming human, and He didn't use His God powers to avoid the pain and hardships of humanity.

Dig Deeper

We can heartily recommend *More Than a Carpenter* by Josh McDowell. It is one of the most popular books (more than eight million copies sold) about the Person of Jesus Christ.

You will get an interesting perspective about Jesus from *The Jesus I Never Knew* by Philip Yancey.

Still skeptical a bit about Jesus? *He Walked Among Us* by Josh McDowell and Bill Wilson presents historical evidence about Jesus.

Moving On

Now that you have a better understanding about who Jesus was, you're ready to examine the circumstances of His life. This is no ordinary biography that you are about to read—not unless you consider a virgin birth, supernatural powers, and death threats to be ordinary.

CHAPTER 2

THE LIFE OF JESUS: FACT OR FICTION?

Whether we are Jew or Christian, believer or atheist, the figure of Jesus—as final Jewish prophet, as innocent and redeeming victim, as ideal human being—is threaded through our society and folded into our imagination in such a way that it cannot be excised. He is the mysterious ingredient that laces everything we taste, the standard by which all moral actions are finally judged.

—Thomas Cahill

There will always be cynics who doubt that certain things in history actually happened. There are people who refuse to believe that astronauts landed on the moon (they think the whole thing was faked on a sound stage). There are those who doubt the Holocaust actually happened. And there are those who don't think Jesus actually lived, or if He did, that He didn't do everything the Bible says He did.

Belief in the Person and work of Jesus isn't like believing in a fairy tale. You can trust what Jesus said and you can believe what He did (including the miracles) because they actually happened. More importantly, they happened for a reason. Find out why in this chapter.

Bruce & Stan

Chapter 2

The Life of Jesus:
Fact or Fiction?

What's Ahead?

➤ Jesus and the People Who Knew Him
➤ More Than a Teacher—But What a Teacher!
➤ What About Those Miracles?

No other person in the history of the world is as famous as Jesus. No other name is so well known, and no other name stirs such emotion as the name of Jesus. These days, famous people come and go like yesterday's news. The great names of the past are a footnote in the history books. But even today, 2000 years after He lived on the earth, Jesus is huge.

The majority of the six billion people living on earth right now know the name of Jesus, and at least a third of all people—more than two billion—identify with Jesus Christ by calling themselves Christians. Yet what do we know about the life of the man from Galilee who called Himself the Son of God? Did Jesus really do everything the Bible says? Did He actually heal the sick, raise the dead, calm the seas, die on a cross, and come back to life again? How do we know if it's all true? And if it's true, what difference does it all make?

In Chapters 3 and 4 we're going to look at the death and resurrection of Jesus, but don't skip ahead! This chapter is going to deal with the life of Jesus, including the people He met, the things He said, and the miracles He performed. We're going to find out if everything happened the way the Bible says, or if some of it is a great story that's been embellished over time.

Jesus and the People Who Knew Him

Jesus said plenty of important things about Himself, but He never wrote anything that started out, "This is the record of My life." Unlike the famous people you read about these days, Jesus wasn't a publicity hound. He wasn't interviewed on local talk shows, such as *Good Morning Palestine,* and He

ONE SOLITARY LIFE

He was born in an obscure village, the child of a peasant woman. He grew up in another obscure village, where he worked in a carpenter shop until he was thirty. Then for three years he was an itinerant preacher.

He never had a family or owned a home. He never set foot inside a big city. He never traveled more than two hundred miles from the place he was born. He never wrote a book or held an office. He did none of the things that usually accompany greatness or success.

While he was still a young man, the tide of popular opinion turned against him. His friends deserted him. He was turned over to his enemies and went through the mockery of a trial. He was nailed to a cross between two thieves. While he was dying, his executioners gambled for the only piece of property he had—his coat. When he was dead, he was taken down and laid in a borrowed grave.

Twenty centuries have come and gone, and today he is the central figure for much of the human race. All the armies that ever marched, and all the navies that ever sailed, and all the parliaments that ever sat, and all the kings that ever reigned, put together, have not affected the lives of people upon this earth as powerfully as this "One Solitary Life."

—adapted from James Allan Francis

never went on a book tour. If anything, Jesus did His best to avoid publicity.

But Jesus did know a lot of people, and a lot of people knew Him. In fact, people were the most important part of His life, especially the people who knew Him but didn't know much about Him. Once, after meeting in the home of a tax collector, Jesus explained His purpose for coming to earth in the first place:

> *And I, the Son of Man, have come to seek and save those like him who are lost* (Luke 19:10).

Jesus didn't come to earth to change history (although He did). Jesus came to change people. Let's take a look at some of the different people Jesus changed.

The Disciples

The people who knew Jesus best were His disciples, handpicked by Jesus (the word *disciple* means "learner" or "follower"). All but one of these 12 ordinary men followed Jesus wholeheartedly. Jesus recruited "the Twelve" after His baptism, which marked the beginning of His public ministry. For the next three years—up until the time He ascended into heaven—Jesus taught this ragtag group, and gradually they learned.

A complete list of these 12 guys can be found in three of the four Gospels (Matthew 10:2-4; Mark 3:16-19; Luke 6:14-16) and in Acts 1:13. Peter, James, and John—who accompanied Jesus at the Transfiguration (Mark 9:2), on the Mount of Olives (Mark 13:3), and in the Garden of Gethsemane (Mark 14:33)—were closer to Jesus than the others. You could say they were in the "inner circle."

One disciple, Judas Iscariot, was the traitor who gave himself over to Satan (John 6:70,71) and betrayed Jesus (this would place him a few notches below Benedict Arnold as the most despicable traitor in history). However, Judas could not have done his dirty work if Jesus had not allowed it (John 13:27). The other seven disciples were Andrew, Philip, Bartholomew, Matthew, Thomas, James (the son of Alphaeus), Thaddaeus, and Simon the Zealot. Matthias was added to the gang after Judas hanged himself and Jesus ascended into heaven (Acts 1:15-26).

WHO WOULD DIE FOR A FAKE?

People who doubt that Jesus was who He said He was need to look at the lives of the disciples. These were all real men who had jobs, families, and a deep belief in God. No mere man claiming to be the Messiah could have had such a profound influence on the disciples. Only Jesus, who claimed to be God in the flesh, could have transformed these ordinary men into bold and powerful proclaimers who turned the world upside down with the message that Jesus was the only way to be saved (Acts 4:12). If Jesus had not been who He claimed to be—if He had been a fake—the disciples would have deserted Him or buckled under the pressure of persecution. But they didn't.

All but one of them was executed for believing in Jesus (and John, the only one who wasn't martyred, was boiled in oil before being banished to the island of Patmos, where he wrote the book of Revelation). The disciples knew Jesus intimately, and they believed He was who He said He was—the Savior of the world, who came to take away the sins of the world (John 1:29).

The Biographers

Two of Jesus' disciples, Matthew and John, were also biographers of Jesus. There were four biographers in all, and all were trustworthy eyewitnesses of the life of Jesus. Lee Strobel quotes Craig Blomberg, one of the most respected authorities on the biographies of Jesus:

> In terms of honesty, in terms of truthfulness, in terms of virtue and morality, these people [the biographers] had a track record that should be envied.

Each biographer wrote from a different viewpoint because each one had a different background, and each told the story of Jesus to a different audience.

- ✓ *Matthew*, a Jewish tax collector, wrote his Gospel (another name for the biography) to prove to his fellow Jews that Jesus was the Messiah.

- ✓ *Mark* wrote his biography to the Romans, who had little interest in the Old Testament prophecies. The Roman mind liked to get to the bottom line, so the Gospel of Mark is short and to the point.

✓ *Luke* was a physician, and probably a Greek, so he wrote to the Greeks and emphasized the human side of Christ's nature.

✓ Because *John* was one of the inner circle, his Gospel is much more personal. The other biographies of Jesus had already been written, so John didn't retell the same details of the life of Jesus. Instead, he chose to focus on seven events and seven sayings to prove that Jesus was God.

What About the Contradictions?

As you read the four Gospels, you will find details that seem to contradict each other. Does this mean the Bible contains contradictions? Not at all. You can trust the Bible because it is God's Word (see *Bruce & Stan's Pocket Guide to Studying the Bible*). God inspired the Bible writers to speak for Him (2 Peter 1:21). God cannot lie (Titus 1:2), and neither can He contradict Himself.

So what do you do with apparent contradictions? Let's look at an example of something that might throw you off. Matthew wrote about one angel appearing to some women on the morning Jesus rose from the dead (Matthew 28:2-5). But in Luke's biography, two angels are mentioned (Luke 24:4). Some people call this a contradiction, but that's not the case at all. Matthew never said there was only one angel. He just said only one angel spoke. Luke wrote about two angels, which doesn't contradict Matthew. The two men are just writing from different perspectives. In fact, the experts say that the differences in perspective validate the truthfulness of the four Gospels rather than deny it. If all the Gospels had been identical, then you could make a case that the four eyewitnesses got together ahead of time to coordinate their stories. "If the gospels were too consistent," Blomberg says, "that in itself would invalidate them as independent witnesses."

The Opposition

It's one thing for the friends and biographers of Jesus to talk and write favorably about Him. You would expect that. But what about those who opposed Jesus, such as the religious leaders? Jesus confronted them and warned His disciples to beware of their false teaching (Matthew 16:11,12). He told the Pharisees and Sadducees that they wouldn't get into the kingdom of heaven because of their hypocrisy (Matthew 23:14).

If anyone had reason to discredit Jesus, it was these people. If there had been any doubts that Jesus spoke with authority, or that His followers were exaggerating His claims, the religious leaders would have jumped on this opportunity to expose Jesus as a fraud. But that never happened. No one ever contradicted the claims and teachings of Jesus. No one ever successfully argued with Jesus and proved Him wrong. All His enemies could do was silence Jesus by putting Him to death, which only served to validate the prophecies concerning the Messiah and accomplish what Jesus came to do.

And what about the demons, those supernatural beings pledged to follow Satan, the number one enemy of God? There were plenty of demons around when Jesus walked the earth, and any one of them could have overpowered Jesus if He had not been the real deal. (Read a story of how some demons jumped on a family of fakes and beat them bloody in Acts 19:13-16.) Yet in every single instance where Jesus confronted a demon or a swarm of demons, they obeyed Jesus as one who had authority over them (Mark 1:27), and they recognized Jesus as "the Holy One sent from God" (Luke 4:34).

The Historians

Even though the Bible is the most reliable and trustworthy ancient document ever written, some people want more evidence for the existence of Jesus. "Show me outside the Bible where it says Jesus lived and walked the earth in first-century Palestine," someone might ask you. Here's what you can tell him.

Josephus was a Jewish historian who lived and wrote in the first century. His writings, which are respected by scholars as accurate, mention Jesus several times, including this paragraph from *Antiquities* quoted by Josh McDowell in *A Ready Defense:*

> Now there was about this time Jesus, a wise man, if it be lawful to call Him a man, for He was a doer of wonderful works, a teacher of such men as receive the truth with pleasure. He drew over to Him both many of the Jews, and many of the Gentiles. He

was the Christ, and when Pilate, at the suggestion of the principal men among us, had condemned Him to the cross, those that loved Him at the first did not forsake Him; for He appeared to them alive again in the third day; as the divine prophets had foretold these and ten thousand other wonderful things concerning Him. And the tribe of Christians so named from Him are not extinct at this day.

Other ancient secular writers—including Cornelius Tacitus and Plinius Secundus—made references to Christ, Christians, and historic events mentioned in the Bible. For example, the first-century historian Phle-gon wrote about the darkness that came upon the earth at the time of Christ's crucifixion.

> *Don't be offended or afraid when people question the objective nature of your faith. In fact, be ready to answer their questions! The Bible says, "And if you are asked about your Christian hope, always be ready to explain it"* (1 Peter 3:15).

More Than a Teacher—But What a Teacher!

Jesus may not be popular in our culture as a Savior, but He ranks pretty high as a great teacher. You see all kinds of books with titles like *The Management Style of Jesus* and *Jesus CEO,* which apply His principles and teachings to the world of business. We even found a book called *The Greatest Psychologist Who Ever Lived,* written by a psychologist who found the teachings of Jesus to be "illuminated, producing profound psychological insights." Nothing wrong with that. After all, Jesus knew human nature better than anyone, so why wouldn't His ideas about success apply to any situation?

What Did Jesus Say?

There's no question that Jesus said some amazingly profound things (you would expect that from God, wouldn't you?), especially in the area of human relationships. Jesus was born into a culture where an oppressive government enslaved people, where women and children were second-class citizens, and where the poor and afflicted were considered less than human. When Jesus declared, "God blesses those who are persecuted" (Matthew 5:10), people couldn't believe it. You mean God actually cares about the downtrodden? As for the persecutors, Jesus had a message no one had ever heard before: "Love your enemies," and "Pray for those who persecute you" (Matthew 5:44).

Jesus raised the moral standards of society as soon as He began teaching, and the world hasn't been the same since. "Love your neighbor as yourself," He said (Mark 12:31). "Whoever wants to be a leader among you must be your servant" (Mark 10:43). Jesus respected women and treated them as equals. He invited children to come to Him and said, "For the Kingdom of God belongs to such as these" (Luke 18:16).

Jesus was the friend of sinners because He came to save sinners. Dallas Willard, who calls Jesus "the smartest man who ever lived," observes, "Jesus took time in his teaching to point out the natural beauty of every human being in the world. Jesus came to obliterate the social and cultural distinctions as a basis for life under God."

What Did Jesus Do?

If all Jesus had done was say a bunch of wise things, then we could rightfully put Him in the same category as Confucius, Benjamin Franklin, or Yogi Berra—people who said stuff that makes you want to stroke your chin and go, "Mmmmm." But what good would that do?

Jesus did more than *say* some very important things. He came to *show* us some very important things:

✓ *Jesus came to show us God's love.* The love of God is the greatest force in the world, because the very essence of God is love (1 John 4:8). The greatest expression of God's love is Jesus, sent by God into a world that has rejected His love. Because God is holy, He can't tolerate our sin. But because God is love, He loves us anyway, and He sent Jesus to show us just how much.

But God showed his great love for us by sending Christ to die for us while we were still sinners (Romans 5:8).

✓ *Jesus came to show us how to love.* A lawyer once asked Jesus to state the most important commandment, and Jesus replied:

"You must love the Lord your God with all your heart, all your soul, and all your mind." This is the first and greatest commandment (Matthew 22:37).

As the greatest expression of God's love, Jesus came to show us how to love God. But that's not all Jesus said about love. Jesus told the lawyer about a second and "equally important" commandment:

Love your neighbor as yourself (Matthew 22:39).

✓ *Jesus came to forgive our sins.* In Chapter 1 we talked about Jesus having the power to forgive sins because He was God. Jesus didn't arrive on planet Earth, look around at all the sin in the world, and decide He needed to offer forgiveness. His plan all along was to forgive sins. That's why He came to Earth in the first place.

And what a difference between our sin and God's generous gift of forgiveness.

For this one man, Adam, brought death to many through his sin. But this other man, Jesus Christ, brought forgiveness to many through God's bountiful gift (Romans 5:15).

✓ *Jesus came to show us how to have eternal life.* All of these wonderful things Jesus came to do—show us God's love, show us how to love, forgive our sins—would have been nice but rather meaningless unless He also came to show us how to conquer death and have eternal life. And that's exactly what Jesus did. Because Jesus died for our sins and rose from the dead, we can have eternal life if we believe in Him. Here's what Jesus said:

I am the resurrection and the life. Those who believe in me, even though they die like everyone else, will live again. They are given eternal life for believing in me and will never perish (John 11:25,26).

What About Those Miracles?

So Jesus said some very important things. So Jesus came to show us some very important things. So what? What difference did it make 2000 years ago, and what difference does it make now? Well, it wouldn't make any difference unless Jesus backed up His claims in a way only God could do. Here's the way Max Anders puts it:

> What Jesus said was so astonishing, what He promised so enticing, what He claimed so magnificent that it simply will not do unless He followed such claims with equally amazing deeds. What good is it for Jesus to offer to forgive sins or bring in the kingdom of God or prepare a home for us in heaven if He were not able to fulfill His words?

The way Jesus backed up His claims was by performing miracles. That's why the four biographies of Jesus are filled with miracles: Jesus turned the water into wine, multiplied food, healed the sick, commanded the weather, and raised the dead. The accounts of Jesus and His miracles aren't like Aesop's fables. They are as real as Jesus Himself.

Why Did Jesus Perform Miracles?

Many people who admire Jesus as a great teacher sneer like intellectual snobs when you bring up His miracles. They get this image of a magician or an illusionist, and they see no connection between the miracles of Jesus and the authority of Jesus. But Jesus didn't set up a big tent and sell tickets so people could see Him do a bunch of tricks. First of all, the miracles of Jesus were real. They actually happened. Secondly, they happened for a purpose—not to entertain, but to help people believe His teaching. Max Anders writes, "Jesus performed miracles to validate the new message of salvation He was bringing to humanity."

Anders illustrates this by looking at the claim Jesus made to forgive sins. (We talked about this in Chapter 1.) Anyone can *say* he can forgive sins, and the religious leaders knew this. They also knew that only God can truly forgive sins (Mark 2:7). When they confronted Jesus with this fact, Jesus agreed. He then healed a paralyzed man in order to prove that He had the authority to forgive his sins, which He had already done (Mark 2:8-11). Not only did Jesus validate His claim, but He also showed that He had power over human frailty and disease.

Another time Jesus was in a boat with His disciples, and a fierce storm threatened their lives. When Jesus calmed the wind and the water simply by commanding them, the disciples were filled with awe. "Who is this man, that even the wind and the waves obey him?" they said. The man was Jesus, who had power over nature.

When Jesus cast out demons, He wasn't just relieving the pain and suffering of possessed individuals. He was demonstrating that He had power over the supernatural world—and Satan himself.

The Miracles Had a Purpose

When the prophet Isaiah foretold the coming Messiah, he wrote:

> *He is coming to save you. And when he comes, he will open the eyes of the blind and unstop the ears of the deaf. The lame will leap like a deer, and those who cannot speak will shout and sing!* (Isaiah 35:4-6).

Jesus knew this, of course, so He embarked on a campaign to do all of those things and more. Every miracle Jesus did had a purpose. Yes, He had compassion on people.

Yes, He wanted to alleviate their suffering. But even more, Jesus wanted to fulfill the Scriptures and prove that He was God in the flesh, able to save humankind spiritually as well as physically.

The teachings of Jesus about love and salvation are very compelling, but it's possible to listen to what Jesus said and put Him on the same level of other great teachers in history. But we can't ignore the miracles of Jesus or say, "Hey, anybody could do that with smoke and mirrors." The miracles invite us to respond, because they show us that Jesus was no ordinary man. They show us that He was the Son of God, equal to God in every way, whose supernatural power can change us from the inside out.

> *What makes us think that we can escape if we are indifferent to this great salvation that was announced by the Lord Jesus himself? It was passed on to us by those who heard him speak, and God verified the message by signs and wonders and various miracles and by giving gifts of the Holy Spirit whenever he chose to do so* (Hebrews 2:3,4).

What's That Again?

1. Even though Jesus is the most famous person in history, we need to know for sure that the details of Jesus' life are true.

2. The disciples and biographers of Jesus, who knew Him best, were trustworthy men who believed Jesus was who He said He was. Even the enemies of Jesus could never prove Jesus wrong.

3. Jesus was a remarkable teacher who said and did some amazing things, but His words and deeds would have been meaningless if He had not backed them up.

4. Jesus backed up His claims by performing miracles, which validated the message of salvation He brought to humanity.

Dig Deeper

One of the best (and bestselling) books about Jesus is *The Case for Christ* by Lee Strobel, a journalist (and former atheist) who investigated the evidence for Jesus.

Max Anders has written a series of books on the basics of the Christian faith (kind of like us). We recommend *Jesus: Knowing Our Savior.*

D. James Kennedy has a wonderful grasp of how Jesus has influenced history. You will be fascinated by his book *What If Jesus Had Never Been Born?*

Moving On

The proof that Jesus lived on earth is undeniable. The words He said, the things He did, and the miracles He performed are living proof that Jesus came to bring salvation to humankind. Is that the end of the story? Is it enough to know that Jesus lived a miraculous life on earth? Well, it's enough to let us know that we need a Savior, but it's not enough to actually save us. Jesus lived His life to show us that we need to be right with God, but He gave His life so we could be right with God. That's what the next chapter is all about.

CHAPTER 3

THE DEATH OF JESUS: WHY DID HE HAVE TO DIE?

It has been the cross which has revealed to good men that their goodness has not been good enough.

—Johann Heironymus Schroeder

You might think it is a bit morbid, but this chapter is all about death. And not just any plain old die-in-your-sleep tranquil kind of death. This chapter is about the painful, hideous, repulsive crucifixion of Jesus Christ.

What makes Christians so obsessed with the death of Jesus? Why is it so special to them when other religions don't celebrate the death of their founders? The answer is simple: The death of Jesus is what makes Christianity work. If there was no cross, there could be no salvation. But salvation (yours and ours) was the reason that Jesus came to Earth. So dying was what Jesus came to do. And because He did it so well, you won't have to.

Bruce & Stan

Chapter 3

The Death of Jesus: Why Did He Have to Die?

Certain symbols are universally recognized. To prove our point, take this little test. See if you can draw the symbol for...

✓ The McDonald's fast-food chain:

✓ Mercedes-Benz:

✓ Zorro:

Here is an even easier one:

✓ Christianity:

To that last one you might have thought of the stick-figure drawing of a fish with the Greek letters *ICHTHYS* inside.

But we are guessing that you aren't fluent in ancient Greek, so you probably identified "the cross" as the symbol for Christianity.

The Symbol of the Cross

While the fish sign is popular as a bumper sticker, the universally recognized symbol of Christianity is the cross. Think about it:

✓ Many women wear necklaces with a pendant in the shape of the cross.

> **Factoid:** The Greek word for fish is ichthys. A fish was one of the earliest symbols for Christianity because the Greek letters for fish were used as an acronym for Iesous Christos Theou Hyios Soter, which is translated into English as "Jesus Christ, of God the Son, Savior."

✓ A cross is on the top of most church steeples.

✓ Many churches have a huge cross hanging on the wall behind the preacher.

✓ When those major league baseball players from the Dominican Republic step to the plate, they make the sign of the cross over their chest.

But why has the cross become the symbol for Christianity? Doesn't the cross represent the defeat of Jesus? Wasn't the cross His lowest point? Why hasn't the empty tomb become the symbol for Christianity? Doesn't the vacant grave represent Christ's triumph over death? Wouldn't that be a better symbol?

Those questions aren't far-fetched. If the tomb wasn't empty—if Jesus hadn't risen from the dead—then He would have been just a mere human who was nothing more than a kook or a crook. But since the tomb was empty, it proved that Jesus was God with power over sin and death, and that proof validated everything He said and taught. (We'll elaborate about the significance of the resurrection in the next chapter.) So, the empty tomb represents a fundamental principle of Christianity. Yet it isn't the traditional symbol. We can think of several reasons why the empty tomb hasn't become the symbol of Christianity:

✓ First of all, the empty tomb wouldn't work design-wise as a pendant or a steeple-topper.

✓ Secondly, imagine how difficult it would be for a baseball player to make the sign of an empty tomb over his chest as he steps into the batter's box.

✓ Thirdly (and seriously), the cross represents the entire purpose and plan for why Jesus came to Earth.

The cross is the climax in each of the biographies of Christ in the New Testament (the books of Matthew, Mark, Luke, and John).

> *Then Jesus began to tell them [the disciples] that he, the Son of Man, would suffer many terrible things and be rejected by the leaders, the leading priests, and the teachers of religious law. He would be killed, and three days later he would rise again* (Mark 8:31).

The cross is central. It is struck into the middle of the world, into the middle of time, into the middle of destiny. The cross is struck into the heart of God.

—Frederick W. Norwood

The cross is all about what Jesus did for you The fact that He was God (as evidenced by the empty tomb) makes what He did the focal point of all human history.

FROM CELEBRATIONS...TO THE COURTS...TO THE CROSS

After three years of public ministry as a teacher, healer, and friend, Jesus went to Jerusalem with His disciples for the Jewish celebration of Passover. These few days preceding His death (called "Passion Week") were tumultuous. The crowds started to acknowledge Him as the Messiah (hoping He would be a military and political leader who could deliver them from Roman oppression). When He rode into Jerusalem on a donkey colt (this is the famous "Palm Sunday" triumphant entry), throngs greeted Him, calling Him "the King of the Jews."

As we discussed in the last chapter, the religious leaders despised Jesus because of His popularity with the people and because His teaching exposed their hypocrisy. These enemies arranged for Him to be falsely arrested. Then they conspired with the Roman governor, Pilate, and ran Jesus through a series of phony trials. They fabricated evidence and violated their own procedural laws. With trumped-up charges, they succeeded in obtaining a death sentence.

The Suffering of the Cross

Death by Roman crucifixion in the first century was not a pretty picture. Somehow, the portrayals that most of us have seen of Christ's crucifixion have been sanitized quite a bit. (Those Easter pageants at church can't get too gory or it might frighten the children.) But the real thing was hideous.

An article in JAMA, the *Journal of the American Medical Association,* reported on the medical aspects of the crucifixion of Christ. Relying on the Bible passages, historical accounts by non-Christian writers, and scientific investigation, the authors reported on the physical effects that Jesus must have endured. Here is a summary of the findings.

The Stress of What He Knew Would Happen

As a man in his early 30s, Jesus was in apparent good physical condition. His travel through Palestine by foot for the prior three years suggests that He had no major physical illness. But as the Passion Week came to an end, Jesus knew that His death was near. Prior to His arrest, He had been praying in the Garden of Gethsemane. He was in great mental anguish. Here is how the disciple Luke (who knew a thing or two about physiology because he was a physician) described it:

> *He prayed more fervently, and he was in such agony of spirit that his sweat fell to the ground like great drops of blood* (Luke 22:44).

The Blindfolded Beating

Jesus was arrested after midnight in the Garden of Gethsemane. Before daybreak, He had endured several phony judicial proceedings and was found guilty of blasphemy. It was at this point that the unmerciful torture began:

> *Then some of them began to spit at him, and they blindfolded him and hit his face with their fists. "Who hit you that time, you prophet?" they jeered. And even the guards were hitting him as they led him away* (Mark 14:65).

The Flogging

Permission for an execution had to come from the governing Romans, so the temple officials took Jesus early in the morning to the residence of Pontius Pilate. Jesus was presented to Pilate not as a blasphemer but rather as a self-proclaimed king who was attempting to subvert Roman authority. On two occasions Pilate found no basis for a legal charge against Jesus (and Herod had come to the same conclusions), but Pilate finally conceded to the protests of the Jewish religious leaders and declared that Jesus be flogged (scourged) and crucified.

By this time, Jesus was probably already in a weakened physical state. He had endured a traumatic and sleepless night, He had been forced to walk more than 2.5 miles to and from the sites of the various trials, and He had endured the beating following His first trial. On top of this, He was now forced to endure a whipping that was particularly sadistic in nature and designed to weaken the victim to a physical state just short of collapse or death.

Jesus was probably stripped of His clothing, with His hands tied to an upright post. Probably two soldiers (taking turns so they wouldn't get tired) flogged his back, buttocks, and legs. The whip used on Jesus probably had a short wooden handle with several single or braided leather thongs of variable lengths, in which small iron balls and sharp pieces of sheep bone were tied at intervals.

✓ The iron balls caused deep contusions, and the leather thongs and sheep bones cut into the skin and subcutaneous tissues.

✓ As the flogging continued, the lacerations tore into the underlying skeletal muscles and produced quivering ribbons of bleeding flesh. The pain and blood loss probably set the stage for circulatory shock.

After the scourging, the Roman soldiers mocked Christ by placing a robe on His shoulders and a crown of thorns on His head, and a wooden staff as a scepter in His right hand. Then they spat on Him and struck Him on the head with the wooden staff. When they tore the robe from His back, they probably reopened the scourging wounds.

The Crucifixion

After the scouring, at about 9 A.M., the soldiers placed Jesus' clothes back on Him

and led Him and two thieves to be crucified. He was made to carry the crossbar of
His own cross (weighing about 75 to 125
pounds), but He faltered. It was carried by
someone else to the hill of Golgotha (also
known as Calvary), about one-third of a
mile away.

At the crucifixion site, Jesus was thrown to
the ground on His back. The scourging
wounds probably tore open again. Tapered
iron spikes about five to seven inches long
were driven through His wrists to nail His
hands to the crossbar. The nails probably
crushed or severed the large median nerve
and produced excruciating bolts of fiery
pain in both arms.

Similar spikes were used to nail His feet to
the vertical post of the cross. Again, nerves
in His feet were injured or severed.

Beyond the agonizing pain, crucifixion was
a form of suffocation. The weight of the
body, pulling down on the outstretched
arms and shoulders, fixed the muscles in
an inhalation state and prevented passive
exhalation. To achieve adequate exhalation,
Christ would have to lift His body by

pushing up on His feet and flexing His elbows and shoulders. This procedure would produce searing pain:

- ✓ Rotating the elbows and shoulders would twist the wrists on the iron nails.

- ✓ Pushing on His feet would drive more weight against the spikes in His feet.

- ✓ Lifting the body painfully scraped His scourged back against the rough wood cross.

By 3 P.M., Jesus died.

Since no one was intended to survive crucifixion, the body of a crucified victim would not be removed from the cross until after the soldiers verified his death. (Sometimes the victim's legs were broken to speed up the process.) By custom, one of the guards would pierce the body with a sword or lance, usually up the right side of the chest to the heart.

With Jesus, the authorities all acknowledged His death, so His legs were not broken. But one soldier pierced His side, probably with an infantry spear.

> *Pilate couldn't believe that Jesus was already dead, so he called for the Roman military officer in charge and asked him. The officer confirmed the fact* (Mark 15:44,45).

The Success of the Cross

Satan probably thought he won when he managed to work through the religious leaders to have Jesus crucified. Maybe Satan and his demons started to party when Jesus breathed His last breath. But the joke was on them. Christ's death on the cross is exactly what God had planned all along. The death of Jesus by crucifixion was the pivotal event that allowed sinful mankind to reconcile with the holy, Almighty God.

The crucifixion of Christ wasn't a tragedy. It wasn't a series of events gone out of control. It was the divinely designed plan of God. Here is an abbreviated list of some of the fundamental accomplishments achieved by Christ's death on the cross.

Each one is a vital part of God's plan of salvation for mankind:

1. Substitution

Christ died so that we don't have to. This is what Christianity is all about, and it required the death of Christ on the cross. It boils down to three basic points:

✓ All humans are sinful.

For all have sinned; all fall short of God's glorious standard (Romans 3:23).

✓ The penalty for our sin is eternal death.

For the wages of sin is death (Romans 6:23).

✓ Jesus was the ultimate human sacrifice. He died in our place.

The law of Moses could not save us, because of our sinful nature. But God put into effect a different plan to save us. He sent his own Son in a human body like ours, except that ours are sinful. God destroyed sin's control over us by giving his Son as a sacrifice for our sins. He did

> *this so that the requirement of the law
> would be fully accomplished for us who
> no longer follow our sinful nature but
> instead follow the Spirit* (Romans 8:3,4).

2. Propitiation

If you're like us, the word *propitiation*
doesn't find its way into your everyday
vocabulary. Theologians use it to explain
that Christ's death on the cross turned God's
wrath away from us. Because God is so holy,
He hates sin and is radically opposed to it.
As sinful beings, that would place us as the
objects of God's wrath. But Christ's death on
the cross appeased God's wrath.

> *For God sent Jesus to take the punishment
> for our sins and to satisfy God's anger
> against us* (Romans 3:25).

3. Reconciliation

God was alienated from mankind because
of sin. That alienation was removed when
Christ died on the cross. Reconciliation
between God and humanity was made
possible.

> *For since we were restored to friendship
> with God by the death of his Son while we*

*were still his enemies, we will certainly be
delivered from eternal punishment by his
life. So now we can rejoice in our wonderful new relationship with God—all because
of what our Lord Jesus Christ has done for
us in making us friends of God* (Romans
5:10,11).

4. Redemption

Before Christ died on the cross, we were
slaves to sin. We were in bondage. We
couldn't escape sin's snare. Think of it as if
Satan had kidnapped you and was holding
you as a hostage. Your release was dependent upon someone paying a ransom.
That's exactly what Christ did on the cross.
He paid the ransom to *redeem* you (literally,
to purchase you back) from Satan. The
ransom price was high. It cost Christ His
life.

*For you know
that God paid a
ransom to save
you from the
empty life you
inherited from
your ancestors.
And the ransom*

> God does not love us
> because Christ died for
> us; Christ died for us
> because God loved us.
>
> —John Stott

> *he paid was not mere gold or silver. He*
> *paid for you with the precious lifeblood of*
> *Christ, the sinless, spotless Lamb of God*
> (1 Peter 1:18,19).

5. Destruction

Satan was behind all of this sin stuff from
the beginning. (Remember the serpent in
the Garden of Eden?) Not only did Christ's
death on the cross free us from Satan's
bondage, it also demolished Satan in the
process.

> *Because God's children are human*
> *beings—made of flesh and blood—Jesus*
> *also became flesh and blood by being born*
> *in human form. For only as a human*
> *being could he die, and only by dying*
> *could he break the power of the Devil, who*
> *had the power of death. Only in this way*
> *could he deliver those who have lived all*
> *their lives as slaves to the fear of dying*
> (Hebrews 2:14,15).

6. Perfection

In the Old Testament times, the priest had
to offer a sacrifice on behalf of the people
each year (in a ceremony referred to as

"the Day of Atonement"). When Christ died on the cross, His sacrifice was enough to cover the sins of all people—past, present, and future.

> *He came once for all time, at the end of the age, to remove the power of sin forever by his sacrificial death for us. And just as it is destined that each person dies only once and after that comes judgment, so also Christ died only once as a sacrifice to take away the sins of many people* (Hebrews 9:26-28).

Salvation comes from what Jesus did without any help from us. He did everything that was necessary. There is nothing else required of us but to accept what He did for us.

The Stumbling Block of the Cross

With all that was accomplished by Christ on the cross, you might think that those first-century Christians had no difficulty in publicizing it. If you think that, you're wrong. The cross was actually the reason that many people rejected Christianity.

The whole concept of salvation through Christ's work on the cross was a stumbling block to many people. Here is how the apostle Paul explained it:

KEY VERSE

I know very well how foolish the message of the cross sounds to those who are on the road to destruction. But we who are being saved recognize this message as the very power of God....God's way seems foolish to the Jews because they want a sign from heaven to prove it is true. And it is foolish to the Greeks because they believe only what agrees with their own wisdom. So when we preach that Christ was crucified, the Jews are offended, and the Gentiles say it's all nonsense (1 Corinthians 1:18,22,23).

Paul was acknowledging that the cross was a big hang-up for a lot of people:

✓ Crucifixion was usually reserved only for slaves, foreigners, revolutionaries, and the vilest of criminals. The Jews didn't want a Messiah who had been humiliated to the point of crucifixion. And the Jews erroneously believed that their good conduct would win

God's favor, so they certainly didn't want a plan for salvation that eliminated the need for their good deeds.

✓ Crucifixion wasn't any more popular with the Greeks. They prided themselves on their intellectualism. They couldn't grasp the concept that a spiritual God would take on an inferior earthly form. The notion seemed absurd to them.

Despite its unpopularity, the cross is the only way to salvation:

> *The fact that I am still being persecuted proves that I am still preaching salvation through the cross of Christ alone* (Galatians 5:11).

Now, 2000 years later, the cross of Christ is still a stumbling block for many people:

✓ Like those first-century Jews, some people today want to earn their salvation. They think that they can please God on their own. With a prideful attitude, they don't want to accept what Jesus did for them because they want to do it themselves.

✓ Others take an intellectual approach
like the Greeks. They want to figure
out their own—usually more compli-
cated—scheme for salvation. They are
offended by the simplicity of it all.

But even Christians have a difficult time
with the cross. They want to forget about
the pain and suffering that Jesus endured.
They want a Jesus who will remove them
from the harsh realities of life. But that isn't
what Jesus is all about.

> *Then Jesus said to the disciples, "If any of
> you wants to be my follower, you must put
> aside your selfish ambition, shoulder your
> cross, and follow me* (Matthew 16:24).

Christ wants us to follow Him. But He
doesn't promise us a life that will be rosy
and without problems. In fact, He
describes it as a life where we will be
carrying our "cross." The term has significant meaning when we understand what
the crucifixion of Christ was all about.

What's That Again?

1. The cross is an appropriate symbol for Christianity because God's entire plan for the salvation of mankind centers on the crucifixion of Christ.

2. Christ endured incredible pain and agony on the cross. He didn't deserve any of it. He was suffering the penalty of sin so that we wouldn't have to.

3. The death of Christ wasn't a failure. It was the successful culmination of God's plan to provide salvation to humanity.

4. Our sins are forgiven by the death of Christ on the cross (as our substitution), which saves us from God's wrath (propitiation), and restores our fellowship with God (reconciliation).

5. With His death, Christ paid the ransom to free us from the bondage of sin (redemption) as He asserted domination over Satan (destruction).

6. There is nothing else required for salvation. The cross did it all (perfection).

7. Some people reject God's plan of salvation because they aren't willing to accept what Christ did for us on the cross.

8. Following Christ requires that we be willing to carry a cross of our own.

Dig Deeper

There are many aspects to Christ. In *100 Portraits of Christ,* Henry Gariepy explains what we can learn about Jesus from His many names and titles.

The information about the physical and medical effects of crucifixion came from "On the Physical Death of Jesus" by William D. Edwards, M.D., Wesley J. Gabel, and Floyd E. Hosmer, as published in the March 21, 1986 issue (Vol. 255, No. 11) of the *Journal of the American Medical Association* (JAMA).

Chapter 13 from *A New Systematic Theology of the Christian Faith* by Dr. Robert L. Reymond or Section X from *Basic Theology* by Charles C. Ryrie will give you an in-depth analysis of the aspects of salvation made possible by Christ's death on the cross.

Moving On

All that Jesus did on the cross would be meaningless if His body remained lifeless in the grave. If He had been a mere mortal, then His death wouldn't have done you any good. Salvation through His death is only possible if He was God. And you know what they say: You can't keep a God-Man down.

CHAPTER 4

THE RESURRECTION OF JESUS: YOU CAN'T KEEP A GOD-MAN DOWN

> *Death, that final curb on freedom, has itself suffered a death blow through the resurrection of Jesus.*
>
> —Michael Green

BRUCE & STAN SAY

Before we look at the resurrection of Jesus, we have to be sure of one thing: Jesus died. If Jesus didn't die, then He merely rose from a swoon or was simply the victim of a hideous prank. But that's not what happened. As we showed you in the last chapter, there is ample historical evidence that Jesus died as a result of crucifixion.

✓ The executioners did not break His legs, as was the custom, because Jesus was already dead.

✓ To be certain that Jesus had died, an executioner jammed a sword in Jesus' side, causing blood and water to pour out. From a medical standpoint, this is a sure sign of death.

✓ Hundreds, if not thousands, of people witnessed the execution of Jesus. Nothing in the historical records shows anything else.

We know Jesus died. Now we'll find out if He rose from the dead.

Bruce & Stan

Chapter 4

The Resurrection of Jesus: You Can't Keep a God-Man Down

. . . .

What's Ahead?

➤ No Resurrection—No Hope
➤ Did the Resurrection Really Happen?
➤ What the Resurrection Means for You
➤ Where Is Jesus Now?
➤ Do You Believe in Jesus?

. . . .

Recently we boarded a plane and were seated on either side of a guy who immediately asked us what we did. We told him that we wrote books about God. Normally this response causes one of two reactions: People either clam up or they want to know more. Much to our surprise, this guy didn't fit into either category. In fact, he didn't really care who we were or what we believed in. He just wanted to tell us about his beliefs, which were rooted in the Baha'i religion.

For the next 20 minutes we had a lively discussion about Baha'u'llah, the leader of the Baha'i faith, who died in 1892. Our new friend (we'll call him Larry) described in detail how difficult it was for the executioners to kill "the Bab" (so named because Baha'u'llah practiced Babism).

"So did he finally die?" we asked Larry.

"Yes, but it took a lot of bullets," Larry replied.

"And is the Bab still dead?" we inquired.

"Well, yes, but his teachings live on," Larry said.

"But the teacher is absolutely dead," we confirmed.

It went on like this for a while. We shared with Larry that we respected his views, but we asked him to consider the life of another great teacher, Jesus Christ, who was also executed, but with one difference. Jesus rose from the dead three days later, and He lives today. We asked Larry if he saw the difference between the Bab and Jesus. We would love to tell you that Larry understood, but we could clearly see that he wasn't at that point in his spiritual journey (the glazed look in his eyes was a clue).

No Resurrection—No Hope

There have been a lot of great teachers throughout history. We don't know much about the Bab, but he was probably a wise person in his own way. So were Confucius, Buddha, and Mohammed. To this day, hundreds of millions of people put their faith in these wise men, but they all died centuries ago. Not one of them rose from the dead—none even claimed that he would come back from the dead. And none of these dead religious leaders—and none others like them who have died—are alive today.

Then there's Jesus. Was He a great teacher? Of course. Did He die? Absolutely. Is He still dead? Absolutely not. Of all the great spiritual leaders or self-proclaimed prophets who ever walked the earth, Jesus is the only one who died and then rose again from the dead.

Now this may not matter to some people (and by the sheer numbers of people who follow dead teachers and prophets, it must not), but it should matter to you. If you are a follower of Christ, you need to know that the resurrection of Jesus is the most important part of your faith. If you are evaluating Christianity against other belief systems, you need to know that Christianity (which is all about Jesus) is no better than Buddhism, Islam, or Baha'i—if Jesus was not raised from the dead. No matter where you are on your own spiritual journey, the resurrection of Jesus is the most important thing you have to deal with.

If there's no resurrection of Jesus from the dead, here's what you're left with:

1. No Resurrection—No Messiah

Throughout the Old Testament, God promised the Jews that He would send a king who would establish God's kingdom on earth. This "deliverer" was referred to as the Messiah. He would be God coming down to earth to save His people. There are more than 40 prophecies concerning the Messiah. The true Messiah must fulfill every single one, including the prophecies that the Messiah would die for the sins of the world (Isaiah 53:7,8), and that God would raise Him from the dead (Psalm 16:9,10). If Jesus did not come back to life after dying, then He wasn't the Messiah. And if Jesus wasn't the Messiah, then both Jews and Gentiles alike (any non-Jew is a Gentile) are still waiting for salvation. As the apostle Paul wrote:

> *And if Christ has not been raised, then your faith is useless, and you are still under condemnation for your sins* (1 Corinthians 15:17).

2. No Resurrection—No Life

Jesus predicted that He would be crucified and then raised from the dead. Speaking about Himself, Jesus said:

> *Then they will hand him over to the Romans to be mocked, whipped, and crucified. But on the third day he will be raised from the dead* (Matthew 20:19).

Jesus didn't just say that He would be resurrected. He also said that He would be the resurrection for us:

> *I am the resurrection and the life. Those who believe in me, even though they die like everyone else, will live again. They are given eternal life for believing in me and will never perish* (John 11:25,26).

If Jesus wasn't raised from the dead, then Jesus was a big fat liar, and there's no hope for us to have eternal life. Without the resurrection, we will "die like everyone else."

3. No Resurrection—No Heaven

Do you think about heaven? There's no loftier thought we human beings can have. Now think about this: Without the resurrection of Jesus from the dead, we'll never get there. Jesus made it very clear that He is our connection to heaven. Not only is He designing and building a place in heaven for all who believe in Him, but He

> No resurrection.
> No Christianity.
>
> —Arthur Michael Ramsey, Archbishop of Canterbury

has also promised to take us there personally:

> *Don't be troubled. You trust God, now*
> *trust in me. There are many rooms in my*
> *Father's home, and I am going to prepare a*
> *place for you. If this were not so, I would*
> *tell you plainly. When everything is ready,*
> *I will come and get you, so that you will*
> *always be with me where I am. And you*
> *know where I am going and how to get*
> *there* (John 14:1-4).

As wonderful and amazing as that sounds,
it doesn't mean a thing if Jesus is still dead.

4. No Resurrection—No Hope

The bottom line is that without the resurrection, we're sunk. Oh yeah, we can
appreciate the teachings of Jesus, we can
do our best to imitate the life of Jesus, and
we can feel good about living good lives
here on earth. But what good is that if
there's no hope of a life with Jesus beyond
this one? If Christians are merely putting
their faith in a dead guy, then they are just
what Ted Turner once called them—a
bunch of losers. Or as the apostle Paul put
it:

> *If we have hope in Christ only for this life,*
> *we are the most miserable people in the*
> *world* (1 Corinthians 15:19).

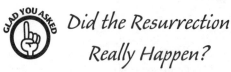 *Did the Resurrection*
Really Happen?

Have we convinced you that the resurrection of Jesus is important to your faith in Christ? It's so important that we want you to know without a shadow of a doubt that it happened just like the Bible said. Yes, you can take God's Word for it, but you can also investigate the facts for yourself and see that they support what the Bible says. That way, if you are ever asked about your Christian "hope" (and we hope that you are), you will be ready to explain it (1 Peter 3:15). Or if you're still looking for hope, you know where to find it.

Here are three proofs for the resurrection of Jesus Christ.

1. The Proof of the Empty Tomb

There's no stronger proof that Jesus rose from the dead than the empty tomb. We know from the Bible and from history that Jesus died. We know that Jesus was buried because a historical character by the name of Joseph of Arimathea—himself a Jew—put the body of Jesus in his own tomb (Matthew 27:57-60). We know that Joseph had a giant stone rolled in front of the entrance (Matthew 27:60), and we know that Pilate sealed the tomb and posted soldiers to guard the tomb at the request of the religious leaders (Matthew 27:62-66). Consequently, if the tomb is empty three days after the death of Jesus, then it stands to reason that Jesus rose from the dead. Or does it?

Ever since the resurrection, people who oppose Christianity have disputed the empty tomb. Here's the reasoning: If you disprove the resurrection by showing that the tomb wasn't really empty—or that it was empty for a reason other than the resurrection—then you can discredit Christianity. We don't disagree. So let's look at the three most popular explanations for the empty tomb (other than the resurrection) and see if they hold water.

Explanation #1: Jesus didn't really die. We have already refuted this theory, but we need to repeat it in this context. There are those who believe that Jesus merely "swooned" from the torture, pain, and exhaustion of the crucifixion, and that He was buried alive. After three days, He was revived by the cool air of the tomb, and walked out under His own power. Of course, if you believe that, then you believe that Jesus not only survived the crucifixion, but was also able to extricate Himself from 70 pounds of tightly wound grave clothes, knock down a 1000-pound rock, and over-power a bunch of armed Roman guards—all without the benefit of food and water for three days.

JESUS CAN'T LIE

Max Anders adds one more objection to this theory. "If Jesus had somehow recovered from a deathlike swoon, He would have been a liar." This would have been completely inconsistent with His character. "Would a person of the integrity revealed in the Gospels have encouraged His followers to preach and base their lives on a lie?" Besides, Jesus is God, and God cannot lie (Titus 1:2).

Explanation #2: The disciples stole the body.
This theory was first proposed by the religious leaders (the very same ones who ordered the crucifixion). Knowing that the resurrection would ignite the Christian movement, they bribed the Roman soldiers assigned to guard the tomb to spread the rumor that the disciples stole the body of Jesus (Matthew 28:12-15). This theory is weak for a couple of reasons. First, it's unlikely that the religious leaders could have convinced all the guards to go along with their little scheme. Second, some of the guards would have certainly noticed the commotion caused by the disciples trying to pry back a huge stone and steal a corpse.

Would You Die for a Lie?

Even if the disciples were able to pull off this amazing feat of strength and daring, why would they die for a lie? Paul Little writes, "Each of the disciples faced the test of torture and martyrdom for his statements and beliefs. People will die for what they *believe* to be true, though it may actually be false. They do not, however, die for what they know is a lie."

Explanation #3: The disciples were hallucinating. One of the proofs of the empty tomb is that hundreds of people saw the resurrected Christ. One of the theories proposed by people who don't believe in the resurrection is that the followers of Jesus were hallucinating. They wanted so much to believe that Jesus was alive that they saw something (or someone) that wasn't really there. This theory has a couple of problems. First of all, the disciples weren't expecting Jesus to rise from the dead (evidently they weren't paying attention when Jesus told them repeatedly that the grave couldn't hold Him). In fact, when reports of the resurrection first came to the disciples, they didn't believe them (Mark 16:11). Second, the same hallucination could not possibly occur to hundreds of people in several locations over a period of 40 days. If anything, such a consistent report from that many people is a proof for the resurrection, not a refutation.

2. The Proof of Hundreds of Eyewitnesses

There's no question that Jesus wanted people to see Him after His resurrection, and hundreds did. The Bible records ten different appearances from the time He rose from the dead until His ascension into heaven 40 days later. He appeared to individuals (such as Mary Magdalene—see John 20:11-18); He appeared to two men walking to Emmaus (Luke 24:13-32); He appeared to the disciples, who couldn't believe their eyes (Luke 24:35-43); and He appeared to more than 500 people at one time (1 Corinthians 15:6). What's interesting about many of these "sightings" is that Jesus had to convince several people that He was really alive by inviting them to touch Him. Read what He said on one occasion to His disciples, who thought they were seeing a ghost:

> *Why do you doubt who I am? Look at my hands. Look at my feet. You can see that it's really me. Touch me and make sure that I am not a ghost, because ghosts don't have bodies, as you see that I do!* (Luke 24:38-40).

3. *The Proof of Transformed Believers*

Once Jesus convinced the disciples that He wasn't a ghost, that He was alive, and that He was going to heaven to prepare a place for them, they went from being frightened weasels to fearless warriors. This is what happens when the living Jesus truly gets ahold of ordinary people, and it's one of the major proofs of the resurrection.

The Book of Acts (the one that follows the four Gospels) tells the dramatic story of these transformed disciples. The Holy Spirit came upon them in power, as Jesus promised (Acts 1:8), and they proclaimed the message that Jesus was alive. Dr. John Walvoord writes:

> The book of Acts would have been meaningless and impossible if it had not been for an actual resurrection of Christ from the dead. The transforming power of Christ witnessed to by Christians through the ages is likewise without explanation if Christ did not actually rise.

The resurrection was the center point of the early Christians. Because they had seen the risen Christ firsthand, they believed and told other people. When the religious leaders tried to stop them, Peter and John replied, "We cannot stop telling about the wonderful things we have seen and heard" (Acts 4:20). And the power of the resurrection didn't stop with just those who saw

Jesus for themselves. In the 2000 years since, it has been the power to change lives.

WHEN SKEPTICS STUDY THE RESURRECTION

Some of the most compelling books ever written about the power of Jesus to change a life were written by people who set out to disprove the resurrection. General Lew Wallace was doing research for a historical novel called *Ben Hur* when he became convinced that the resurrection was true. Frank Morison wrote *Who Moved the Stone?* after his research showed him the validity of the resurrection. C.S. Lewis was one of the most vocal and articulate skeptics in this century, but he became one of the most convincing converts because he couldn't deny the evidence for the resurrection. Josh McDowell thought he could disprove the resurrection, but ended up in the opposite camp. He has written several books showing proofs for the resurrection. Our favorite is *More Than a Carpenter.*

What the Resurrection Means for You

The resurrection is an event that happened in history, but in order for its power to take hold in your life, you need to take it personally. Because of the resurrection, here's what Jesus can do for you.

Jesus can save you.

The very name *Jesus* means "the Lord saves" (Matthew 1:21). The resurrection gives credibility and power to the name. Because Jesus was raised to life, it means that Jesus can save you by bringing you back into a relationship with God (this is what it means to "get right" with God). In fact, believing in the resurrection is the prerequisite to your salvation.

For if you confess with your mouth that Jesus is Lord and believe in your heart that God raised him from the dead, you will be saved (Romans 10:9).

Jesus can conquer death for you.

Not only can Jesus save you and restore you to a right relationship with God, but He can also save you from the eternal consequence of sin, which is death (Romans 6:23).

> *For since we were restored to friendship with God by the death of his Son while we were still his enemies, we will certainly be delivered from eternal punishment by his life* (Romans 5:10).

Jesus can give you eternal life.

If the only hope we have is in this life, then we are "the most miserable people in the world" (1 Corinthians 15:19).

> *But the fact is that Christ has been raised from the dead. He has become the first of a great harvest of those who will be raised to life again* (1 Corinthians 15:20).

The resurrection of Jesus guarantees our resurrection. "He is able to bestow eternal life by virtue of who He is and what He has done in His death and resurrection," writes John Walvoord. Wow! What a benefits package. This isn't like going to work for a company that promises all sorts of perks and bonuses, and then goes out of business, leaving you high and dry with worthless stock options. The fact that Jesus

rose from the dead guarantees God's
promise to save you now and give you
eternal life in the future.

Where Is Jesus Now?

The Bible gives us a detailed account of
what Jesus did while He was on earth. But
what happened to Him after He rose from
the dead, and what has He been doing
since then? We know that between the time
of His resurrection and His ascension into
heaven (Acts 1:9-11), Jesus hung around for
40 days, showing Himself to hundreds of
people and giving His disciples final
instructions. Jesus is in heaven now, "in the
place of honor next to God, and all the
angels and authorities and powers are
bowing before him" (1 Peter 3:22). Does
this mean Jesus is no longer here on earth
with us? Not in body, but He is here spiritually, living in all who have invited Him
into their lives (Colossians 1:27).

What Is Jesus Doing?

Just because Jesus is at the right hand of
God doesn't mean He is sitting around,
biding His time until He returns to earth in
the Second Coming. Jesus is engaged in at

least three different very important activities, all of which concern you:

1. *Jesus is preparing a place for you.* You can be sure that Jesus is engaged in the most spectacular construction project in the history of the universe: He's preparing heaven...for you (John 14:2).

2. *Jesus is praying for you.* Actually, the Bible says that Jesus is "pleading" to the Father on your behalf. Who better to plead your case before God? No one knows you better than Jesus (Hebrews 4:15,16).

3. *Jesus is keeping the universe going for you.* There's a reason why the universe functions so beautifully: Jesus is holding all creation together (Colossians 1:17).

He'll Be Back

There's one final thing Jesus has promised to do, and that's to come to earth a second time (that's why they call it the Second Coming). Jesus said, "When everything is ready, I will come and get you, so that you will always be with me where I am" (John 14:3). This isn't a fairy tale. This is real.

And it's the most exciting prospect you could ever have in life, made possible by the resurrection of Jesus Christ.

> *Now we live with a wonderful expectation because Jesus Christ rose again from the dead* (1 Peter 1:3).

Do You Believe in Jesus?

Throughout this book we have been talking about the Person of Jesus, the life of Jesus, the death of Jesus, and the resurrection of Jesus. You've read about Jesus from front to back. You don't know everything there is to know about Jesus, but you know quite a bit. At this point we don't have any more to say, but we have one question: Do you believe in Jesus?

Before you answer that, you need to know that your belief is directly related to the level of your faith. If you believe that Jesus lived and died and rose from the dead in history, then you have a faith based on *knowing who Jesus is*. This is an essential step of faith, but it's not the only step.

If you believe that Jesus is the Son of God and the only way to get into a right relationship with God, then you have a faith based on *agreeing with what Jesus said*. You move from believing in Jesus to believing Jesus. This is another essential step of faith, but there's one more step.

The final step of faith is to make a decision to personally depend on Jesus for your salvation. This is when your faith is complete, because it is based on *receiving what Jesus did*. This is when you move beyond mere belief in the facts to a personal trust in Jesus to save you.

When you find Someone this trustworthy— especially when your life depends on it— you grab onto Him. You don't just *know* about Jesus; you don't just *agree* with Jesus; you make a decision to *receive* Jesus and follow Him fully.

For God so loved the world that he gave his only Son, so that everyone who believes in him will not perish but have eternal life (John 3:16).

What's That Again?

1. Jesus is the only religious leader who died and came back to life and lives today.

2. The resurrection of Jesus is the most important part of your faith.

3. Without the resurrection, there is no Messiah, there is no eternal life, there is no heaven, and there is no hope.

4. There are at least three historical proofs for the resurrection of Jesus: the empty tomb, hundreds of eyewitnesses, and the transformation of believers.

5. More than a historical event, Jesus can personally change your life because of the resurrection. He can save you, He can conquer death for you, and He can give you eternal life.

6. Jesus is in heaven right now preparing a place for you, praying for you, and keeping the universe going for you. Oh, and He's coming back for you as well.

7. True faith involves knowing who Jesus is, agreeing with what Jesus said, and receiving what Jesus did.

Dig Deeper

There are three more books we want to recommend. Each one has some excellent information on the resurrection of Jesus.

Know Why You Believe is a classic book by Paul Little. The chapter entitled "Did Christ Rise from the Dead?" is one of the clearest you'll ever read.

What Is the Proof for the Resurrection? by Ralph Muncaster is a booklet in his Examine the Evidence series. Lots of charts, verses, and history.

Jesus Christ Our Lord by John Walvoord is a classic study on the Person and work of Christ. This one is almost a seminary level text, but don't let that deter you. It's good to stretch your mind once in a while.

Moving On

More books have been written about Jesus Christ than about any other person in history, and we feel privileged to have added one more to the list. But what's one more book about Jesus unless it makes you think about Jesus on a personal level? Somehow we think that's already happened, because you can't just stop with what Jesus taught. You have to deal with who He is and what He did for you.

As C.S. Lewis observed, Jesus leaves you very few options. Either He was telling the truth or He wasn't. If He wasn't telling the truth, then He must have been a liar or a lunatic. If He wasn't a liar or a lunatic, then He was telling the truth. And if Jesus was telling the truth, then He is who He said He was, which leaves you with a decision. What do you do with Jesus? How will you respond to the truthful claims—and the personal invitation—of Jesus Christ, who says:

> *Look! Here I stand at the door and knock. If you hear me calling and open the door, I will come in, and we will share a meal as friends* (Revelation 3:20).

About the Authors

Bruce Bickel is a lawyer, but he didn't start out that bad. After college, he considered the noble profession of a stand-up comic, but he had to abandon that dream because he is not very funny. As a lawyer, he makes people laugh (but it is not on purpose).

Stan Jantz is a retail-marketing consultant. From the time he was a little kid, Stan's family owned a chain of Christian bookstores, so he feels very comfortable behind the counter.

Bruce and Stan spend their free time as "cultural observers" (they made that term up). They watch how God applies to real life. Together they have written more than 25 books.

Other Books by the Guys:

Bruce & Stan's® Guide to God
Bruce & Stan's® Guide to the Bible
Bruce & Stan's® Guide to How It All Began
Bruce & Stan's® Pocket Guide to Talking with God
Bruce & Stan's® Pocket Guide to Sharing Your Faith
Bruce & Stan's® Pocket Guide to Studying the Bible
Bruce & Stan's® Pocket Guide to Knowing Jesus
God Is in the Small Stuff (and It All Matters)
Real Life Is a Contact Sport
Real Life Has No Expiration Date
Bruce & Stan's Search for the Meaning of Life

Bruce and Stan would enjoy hearing from you. (If you've got something nice to say, then don't hold back. If you have a criticism, then be gentle.) The best way to contact them is:

E-mail: **guide@bruceandstan.com**
Snail Mail: Bruce & Stan
P.O. Box 25565
Fresno, CA 93729-5565

You can learn more than you ever wanted to know about Bruce and Stan by visiting their Web site: **www.bruceandstan.com**